relaX

relaX

200 ways to achieve calm in mind and body
Renata and Steven Ash

THUNDER BAY
P·R·E·S·S

San Diego, California

DESIGNER: Mark Buckingham DESIGN MANAGER: Justina Leitão EDITOR: Jane Alexander
ILLUSTRATIONS, SCANNING & RETOUCHING: Mark Buckingham
PRODUCTION: Neil Randles, Karen Staff

Thunder Bay Press
An imprint of the Advantage Publishers Group
5880 Oberlin Drive, San Diego, CA 92121-4794
www.advantagebooksonline.com

© Salamander Books Ltd 2002

A member of Chrysalis Books plc

All notations of errors or omissions should be
addressed to Thunder Bay Press, editorial
department, at the above address. All other
correspondence (author inquiries, permissions)
concerning the content of this book should be
addressed to Salamander Books Ltd. 8 Blenheim
Court, Brewery Road, London N7 9NY, United
Kingdom.

Library of Congress Cataloging-in-Publication Data
Ash, Renata.
  Relax: 200 ways to achieve calm in mind and body/Renata and Steven Ash
    p. cm.
  ISBN 1-57145-566-3
  1. Stress (Psychology) 2. Stress management. 3. Relaxation. I. Ash, Steven. II. Title.
BF575.S75 A74 2001
155.9'042-dc21

2001052264

Produced by Toppan
Printed in China
3 4 5 02 03 04

*This book is not intended to be a substitute
for professional or medical advice or care,
and any user of this book should always
consult a licensed physician before adopting
any particular course of treatment.*

contents

chapter 1

feel good

about yourself

is stress good for you?

Stress can be defined as anything which makes a demand on us to respond. But it is our response to stress that is important in terms of our health. If a stressful situation causes anxiety, tension, raised blood pressure, and so on, over a period of time it can lead to illness. Another person, who responds to the same pressures with a relaxed, no-sweat attitude may not suffer ill effects.

It may be difficult to believe, but some stress is actually good for you. Positive stress is what you feel after a rewarding week at work, or a successful day's shopping. You may feel tired, but after a rest you will be refreshed and pleased with your achievements. Positive stress provides essential stimulus or motivation, and without it boredom can set in. Viewed as challenges or opportunities, tasks generate stimulating stress; viewed as threats, the same tasks generate negative stress.

the stress test

This table lists a number of major life events and assigns them a value according to the level of stress they engender. A score of more than 150 shows you need to take extra care of yourself, and over 300 means stress is likely to affect your health unless you manage it effectively.

Major Life event	Stress level
Death of spouse	100
Divorce	73
Marital separation	65
Jail term	63
Death of close family member	63
Personal injury or illness	53
Marriage	50
Loss of job	47
Marital reconciliation	45
Retirement	45

positively,
positively
thoughtful

The glass is either half full or half empty, depending on our attitude. We may not be able to control what happens to us throughout our lives, but we can control our thoughts and reactions to these events. Instead of constantly looking for the worst in everything, we can begin to look at what opportunity it might provide. When we are faced with a particular challenge, we can either give ourselves wings to fly by saying "I can" or tie ourselves to the ground with a ball and chain by telling ourselves "I can't." Maybe we will surprise ourselves with how high we can fly!

blow a
fuse

and release
pent up
anger

Human
beings are equipped with a wonderful
mechanism, called "flight or fight," which must have
served our forefathers incredibly well when confronted with
ferocious animals. We live in a different world. Our opponent is not
a wild animal—it is an arrogant boss, a nagging partner, or an unruly
child who keeps our adrenalin levels topped up. You cannot punch
your boss on the nose, but you can equip yourself with a
punchbag—even a simple mattress or a firm pillow will
do—and fight it to your heart's content. Just pretend it
is your boss, and notice how you feel
after your "workout!"

smile

and bring the **magic** back

into your life

The simple action of smiling stimulates the release of powerful neuropeptides, which are responsible for feelings of happiness, joy, and peace. So remind yourself to smile more often, even if it's for no reason whatsoever! Smiling reminds you that you are more than just your problems. It reminds you that you are beautiful and everything is OK just the way it is.

quote:

my motto is the same as my blood type: B Positive.

Cynthia Nelms

whatever you can do,
or dream you can, begin it;
boldness has genius,
power, and magic in it.

Goethe

Imagine setting off on a journey without really knowing where you are going. Chances are you will get lost or just drive around aimlessly and return frustrated and tired at the end of the day. Our lives are a constant journey. To achieve our dreams we have to turn them into goals. Give yourself time to find out what you really want. Then set your goals and keep your mind focused on them. Your goals will act as the signposts to keep you on track.

set

goals

every moment of your life
is infinitely creative
and the universe is endlessly bountiful.

Shakti Gawain

Take your courage in your hands and be creative. Life holds so many wonders and opportunities when you look through the eyes of creativity. You do not have to be an artist; creativity can be as simple as cooking a meal for your family, or redecorating your room. It can also mean joining an art class and trying painting or drama. And it is never too late to discover your musical talents, especially if you have always been told you can't sing. Life is a constant process of creation and we will only be truly fulfilled and happy when our own creativity is allowed to express itself.

23

For most of us, clothes rank high in the list of things we do not want to let go of. But this creates clutter and, according to the principles of Feng shui, clutter leads to stagnation. You might have bought that expensive suit only a year ago, but if you since have grown a size bigger and are struggling with your weight, give the suit to a thrift shop or throw it out and concentrate on the present. It is much better to have only items in your closet which you can really enjoy and feel good in. That way you add lightness and happiness to your life instead of stress and guilt.

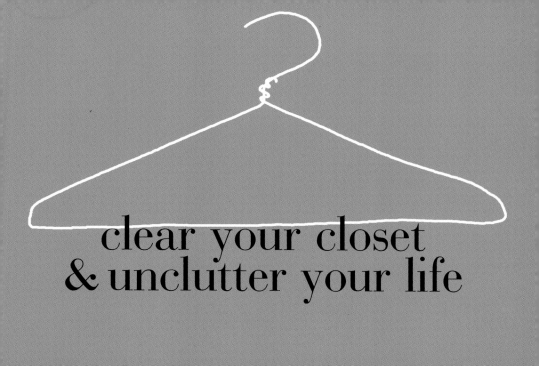

clear your closet
& unclutter your life

st. john's wort: the herbal prozac?

Nature has got a potent answer to anxiety, restlessness, and depression—herbalists have been using St. John's Wort to treat these conditions for centuries. It has recently been clinically tested, and reports on its benefits are so good it is now Germany's top prescription choice for treating mild depression. As with all natural remedies, results are not instant but improvements are usually felt within two to three weeks. The oil of this wonderful healing plant can be taken internally to treat gastritis and gastric ulcers—another painful reminder to reduce the stress in our lives.

We are often our own worst enemies, and this exercise will help redress the balance. When encountering difficulties at work, with your family or with friends, imagine you are your best friend. Give yourself the support, sympathy, perspective and encouragement you would if you were your best friend. Listen to the advice you are giving. It should be gentle, caring, and encouraging. Does it vary from the way you usually speak to yourself?

be your own

best

friend

for a week

mood food:

eat your greens

When you are under stress, the body consumes more nutrients, so it is vital to eat well even if this is the last thing you feel like doing. B vitamins, found in whole grains, green vegetables, eggs, pulses, nuts, seeds, meat and fish, help release energy from food and maintain a healthy nervous system. Vitamin C, found in fresh fruit and vegetables, helps resist infection, as does zinc, which is found in egg yolk, dairy produce, liver, red meats, and seafood. Whole grains, wholewheat pasta, root vegetables, and potatoes will boost energy levels and complete your stress-busting diet.

warm butternut squash salad

1/2 lb butternut squash

7-8 tablespoons olive oil

coarse sea salt

*1 cup each shredded young spinach
    and green cabbage*

1 small kohlrabi, cut into strips

3 tablespoons pumpkin seeds

1 tablespoon wine vinegar

2 tablespoons orange juice

Cut the squash in half crosswise and peel remove the seeds and fibers. Slice and fry in batches until lightly brown. Sprinkle with sea salt, and put in a colander to drain. Arrange the spinach, cabbage, kohlrabi, and pumpkin seeds on plates and top with the squash. Heat the oil from the squash with the vinegar and orange juice, pour over the squash, and garnish. Serve warm.

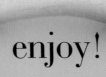

enjoy!

Keep a journal every morning and get it all off your chest. Write down all your fears, worries, gripes, plans, hopes, and dreams. Expressing yourself in a safe way like this can clarify exactly what it is you want and where you are struggling in life. Write at least three pages every morning. If you feel resistance to the idea, look at the resistance, and then continue. Don't sabotage yourself! Getting all your thoughts down on paper can give you an entirely new perspective on life.

our sphere of action is life's happiness

John Wilmot

Take a pen and write down ten things that you enjoy doing. These could be as various as walking in the rain, going to concerts, eating popcorn, making love, rollerblading, making cookies, dancing, or painting. Then ask yourself when you last had fun just for you. Pick one of the things from your list and do it. Having fun is one of the most relaxing things you can do.

astern cultures state that a sense of enjoyment opens our bodies to the nourishment provided by food; in the West, we would say that if we are relaxed the digestive process works better. It all amounts to the same thing. Eating good, healthy food is one of the most enjoyable relaxations we have available, so make the most of it! Eat with other people when you can for maximum enjoyment. Take your time, sit around the table, and enjoy!

making
the most
of food

blow
your
own
trumpet

We learn behavior and communication skills as we grow which influence how we learn to interact with others. Circumstances in our childhood may have taught us certain behavioral patterns such as aggression, manipulation, subserviency or trying to please everyone. These old ways of responding can be major sources of stress in our lives. Assertiveness is about communicating and behaving in ways that offer the most effective and least stressful outcomes. An assertive approach carries no hidden messages and is easy for the listener to interpret—and reduces stress.

Tick each statement if you agree with it, and add a second tick if this is how you currently behave. The more double ticks, the more assertive you are. If there are only single ticks, consider taking an assertiveness training course.

It is OK to state your needs irrespective of what others expect of you.

It is OK to state your needs.

It is OK to make mistakes and admit to these.

It is OK to change your mind.

If you want something, you have the personal right to ask for it.

You respect and honor anyone else who exercises these same rights.

test your
assertiveness

flower power

Dr Bach to the rescue

The most frequently used of all the flower remedies, Rescue Remedy is a powerful combination of five Bach remedies. It is helpful whenever you are feeling stressed. It eases panic and anxiety, and can help you to face a difficult interview, exams, or the dentist. Keep it in your pocket to help deal with unexpected crises more easily. You can dab it on stings, strains, and bruises to ease the pain. It's also excellent for children when they are having a panic attack or a tantrum; simply rub it on their temples or wrists, there's no need for them to ingest it. For adults, it can also be given in a glass of hot water, which will help to disperse the alcohol. If you're giving a talk or presentation, sip the glass of water if you feel the return of fear or tension.

Juices you prepare yourself are bursting with quickly absorbed enzymes, vitamins, and minerals, and play a vital role in promoting health and vitality. Drink regularly for a convenient and potent cocktail of nutrients. Make sure your ingredients are absolutely fresh, and use organic produce if possible, because it does not contain any harmful pesticide residues. Use a centrifugal juicer for the best results.

Apple and grape juice is a vitamin C-rich juice which helps resist infection and is very simple and quick to prepare. Simply juice 2 fresh crisp apples, 3 tablespoons fresh lemon juice, and 3 ounces seedless green grapes. This juice oxidizes quickly, so drink it immediately after juicing. Serves 1.

juice
for joy!

chapter 2

gentle awakenings

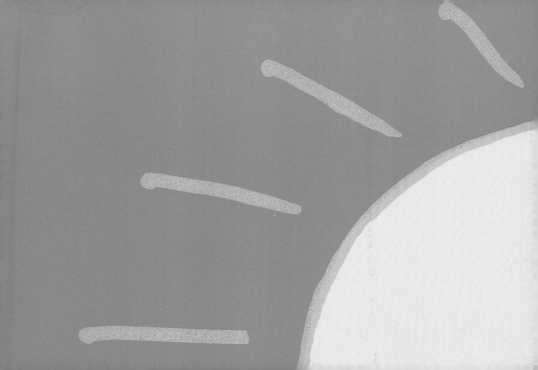

The way we start out in the morning can set the pattern for the rest of the day. Therefore it makes sense to center ourselves at the beginning of the day to make the best of all the opportunities it holds. Upon waking, gently stretch your body and enjoy the feeling of being alive. As you look ahead toward this day, see yourself handling your tasks in a totally positive way. Visualize as clearly as you can each situation, turning it into the best outcome you can imagine for it. See yourself relaxed, happy, and confident, and capable of achieving whatever needs to be done. Enjoy the feeling of total satisfaction and success in every area of your life before getting up and starting your daily routine.

breakfast

and

early

morning meals

Breakfast, however simple, can be an enjoyable and therapeutic ritual. Taking time for it, rather than running around in a frantic state, creates a sense of order, and gives you the chance to calmly contemplate the hours ahead. Breakfast usually follows a long period of fasting during sleep, so it is important to refuel, otherwise you may feel lethargic and jaded by midmorning. You don't have to eat a substantial breakfast, but do eat a sustaining one. Breakfast can consist of anything you like, but the bare essentials are a whole grain—either in breakfast cereal or wholewheat toast—or fresh fruit, or a small pot of plain yogurt.

Coffee, tea, and cola drinks are all loaded with caffeine. This gives a temporary lift, but caffeine can cause nervousness, headaches, trembling, irritability, and palpitations, and it depletes the body of vitamins. Herbal teas have been drunk for thousands of years, and make an enjoyable and healthy substitute. They can also help cleanse, calm, or stimulate the body in a gentle but effective way, and can be taken according to your need, mood, and the season.

cut the caffeine

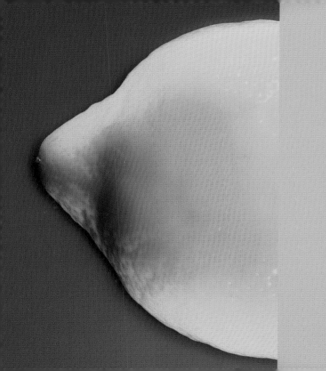

herbal
teas
for a
gentle
start to
the
day

Lemon Herb Tea

For a wonderfully refreshing but gentle tea which isn't too much of a shock to the system, add a good handful of fresh, washed lemon balm, lemon verbena, or bergamot leaves, or a mixture of all three, and 1–2 bruised lemongrass leaves or stalks to a teapot of boiling water and brew for 5 minutes. Strain into a cup and serve.

Ginger and Mint Tea

Ginger and mint have a stimulating aroma and settle the stomach. Rinse a good handful of fresh mint leaves, peel and thinly slice a 1-inch piece fresh ginger, and put in a 2-cup teapot of boiling water. Infuse for 5 minutes, then strain.

Hot Pear Juice with Cardamom

Crush seeds from 4 green cardamoms, and boil with $2\frac{1}{2}$ cups water for five minutes. Strain into a cup containing 2 tablespoons pear juice concentrate. This is less acidic and kinder to an empty stomach than cold fruit juice.

Listening to the news is usually a depressing and debilitating experience. It saps our energy by telling us about all the terrible things that have happened in the world which we are powerless to change. Gently start listening to the news on the radio less often, and reduce the number of newspapers you read. If you read a newspaper every day, begin by cutting it down to twice a week, and give yourself a rest from bad news. Turn off the TV when the bad news appears, and instead start your day with some gentle music. You'll feel better and you may find you can give up news altogether once you get into the swing of it.

quote:

at any moment
I could start being
a better person

but which moment
should I choose?

Ashleigh Brilliant

There are more than 400 skeletal muscles inside the body and each one contracts when it is working and lengthens when it is relaxed. You feel vibrant after you have stretched and exercised because of the increased oxygen flow throughout your body. Stretching reduces muscular tension, while increasing the blood and oxygen flow. When you wake up, allow your body to gently stretch out. Breathing deeply and slowly, find the natural limit for each limb in as many directions as possible, moving slowly and gracefully. Smile and let the smile bathe all the tissues, preparing you for a new day.

gentle stretchings

ombine all the dry ingredients in a bowl. Beat in the buttermilk, egg, and oil. Heat a griddle or heavy-based skillet and brush with a little oil. Pour 2 tablespoons onto the griddle, spreading it with the back of a metal spoon to form a 4-inch circle. Add 3 or 4 more circles, depending on the size of your pan. Fry for 30 seconds, or until holes start to appear on the surface. Flip the pancakes over and fry on the other side for 30 seconds, or until golden brown. Keep warm while you make the rest. Top with a spoonful of yogurt and honey and serve with fresh berries or warm applesauce.

buckwheat pancakes

¾ cup buckwheat flour

¾ cup all-purpose flour

1 teaspoon sugar

½ teaspoon baking powder

½ teaspoon baking soda

¼ teaspoon salt

1½ cups buttermilk

1 large egg, beaten

1 tablespoon grapeseed or
  safflower oil

honey, plain yogurt, and fresh
berries or warm applesauce,
to serve

Walking is one of the most popular and beneficial forms of physical exercise. It helps access more energy by calming the mind and energizing the body. Making a brisk walk part of your daily routine will improve your sleep, digestion, and muscle tone. It will exercise your heart and lungs without overstraining the body. You will also find yourself being more relaxed and happy. By focusing energy in your body instead of in your head you allow yourself to switch off from your everyday problems and worries.

walking back
to happiness

start your day with a stimulating aromatic bath

Add three drops of bergamot, three drops of petitgrain, and two drops lemon essential oil to a bath of warm water for a truly invigorating start to the day. Run a warm rather than a hot bath because hot water is debilitating, even though it does feel good. Petitgrain essential oil is derived from the leaves and twigs of the bitter orange tree and is relaxing as well stimulating and will counteract any tendency to early-morning sluggishness.

Look to this day;
For it is life,
The very life of life.
In its brief course lie all
The realities and verities of existence,
The bliss of growth,
The splendor of action,
The glory of power—

For yesterday is already a dream,
And tomorrow is only a vision.
But today, well lived,
Makes every yesterday a dream of happiness
And every tomorrow a vision of hope.
Look well, therefore, to this day:

"
a Sanskrit
proverb
"

get up earlier

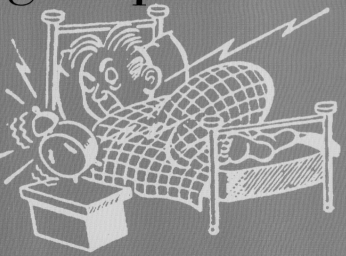

One of the most important things to combat stress is to start your day in a relaxed, peaceful way. Rushing out of bed at the last minute, skipping breakfast, and racing to work or rushing your children to school is bound to make the rest of the day as stressful as its beginning. One way of combating this "early-morning stress syndrome" is to actually make a habit of getting up half an hour earlier. This will give you the time to get up in peace and maybe ponder quietly the tasks of the day ahead and how you plan to handle them.

old water is nature's greatest cleanser, and its revitalizing effect on the system has been known since the times of Paracelsus. The skin, the body's largest endocrine organ, is toned and stimulated by cold water. It drives the blood from the periphery into the vessels deep in the muscles and is exceptional exercise for the skin and circulation. After you have taken the plunge the initial feeling of shock is quickly replaced by a wonderful sense of relaxation and well-being as your blood starts to move back to the surface.

mood colors

Close your eyes and imagine you are walking in a beautiful garden. It is a bright sunny day and all the flowers are in full bloom. Let your eyes rest on the magnificent display of colors—how do you feel?

Research shows that colors do have distinct influences on our emotional and physical well-being. So why not make use of these findings by incorporating them into your life? Wear cooling blue or purple, or balancing green when you feel uptight and wound up. If the day ahead seems all gloomy and depressing, brighten your mood with clear reds and warm yellows. Bright orange and gentle peach colors can help kick-start your creative talents and give you the self-confidence you need to make this day your day!

a brighter you

quote:

*music is the greatest power
I have ever experienced. I doubt if
anything else equals its power to act
upon the human organism.*

Jean Maas

xperiments show that plants exposed to heavy rock music grow away from the speakers and can even wither up and die, while seedlings exposed to Bach grow toward the speakers, and grow more rapidly than control plants. Tests show music also has profound effects on the human physiology, slowing the heart and breathing rate, lowering blood pressure, improving immune function, and balancing hormone levels. Slow, soothing melodies are preferable to fast, upbeat sounds. As with plants, Baroque music seems to have the most beneficial effect, but to experience the benefits of music it is most important you find music that you like and relate to.

take a
supplement

Stress can adversely affect the way your body processes food, and in stressful times we often give less attention to diet and general lifestyle. While supplements are not a substitute for a well-balanced diet, they are certainly useful to guarantee your body gets all the nutrients it needs on a daily basis. A well-balanced multivitamin and mineral supplement is the safest way to take supplements. Antioxidants such as vitamins B, C, E, A, and beta carotene, are particularly good in protecting your body from the effects of a stressful lifestyle and a bad diet, as well as selenium, certain enzymes, and phytonutrients. If you are unsure about your needs, consult a qualified nutritionist.

make it your day: how to plan for 24 stress-free hours

make a
list

aking a list of things you have to do ranks high in the recommendations of stress-management trainers all over the world. To put down in writing what you want to achieve in any given day ties in with the habit of goal setting. It also takes away a lot of the stress that comes with constantly holding in your mind the tasks that need to be tackled.

When writing your list, put the most important items at the top and be reasonable about what you expect to complete. Keep reviewing your list throughout the day, and don't forget to tick off the items that have been dealt with. At the end of the day return to your list again and congratulate yourself on your achievements.

changing your

It is a good idea to examine your behavior patterns and recognize the things that cause the most stress in your life. For example, if you find yourself saying yes too often when you really would rather decline, it is important for you to identify this behavior as a major cause of distress and energy depletion, and resolve to take action to change it now.

Make a list of all the things you don't want to do any more, because you have recognized their detrimental effect on your health and well-being. Put this list in a very obvious place in your home, perhaps on the bathroom mirror or the refrigerator door. It will help you to keep on the right track and avoid unnecessary stresses.

behavior patterns

quote:

*humor is a whisper
from the soul,
imploring mind and
body to relax,*

let go, and be at peace again.

Anon.

Can you remember how easy it was to find things funny when you were a child? As grown-ups we seem to have forgotten how to have fun. But the child within you is still alive, waiting to look through your eyes with the excitement and wonder of innocence.

have
fun

Make a date with yourself and take the time to sit quietly in order to meet the person that you have become. Maybe your dreams have changed and you need a new direction. Maybe you need to spend more time with your partner or children, because your family routine has started to fall apart unnoticed. Maybe your own health and fitness routine has become stale and you need to find a new form of exercise that will allow you to feel good in your body again. Whatever it is that you need to change, discover it and do it!

Being assertive about your own space and acting in *your* best interest may be one of the most effective stress-reducing strategies you can adopt. The fact is you cannot please everybody. Constantly giving into other people's demands to the detriment of your own peace of mind and well-being does not really benefit anyone. It puts a strain on friendships and relationships, as well as undermining your self esteem.

Practice listening to your inner voice more and follow through even if it means saying "no." That way you let others know your boundaries and they will respect you for it.

learn to listen to your inner voice

Every person is different! This is also true of our internal clocks. Whereas some people are able to get up bright and early and immediately switch into working mode, others may take until late morning to get their energy going. On the other hand, the late starters are often able to work until late at night with their peak performance at around midafternoon, whereas the early birds have expended all their energy by that time. This phenomenon is due to our internal regulating systems called biorhythms.

To get the best out of your day, get to know your inner clock. Then you can plan ahead and tackle the most important activities of the day at your peak-performance time.

work
within
your best
time
limits

*when one is engaged in
a favorite pursuit or a subject that is
absorbingly interesting, the normal
conception of labor or time
and artificial social distinctions
disappear from the mind.*

G. Koizumi (Judo master)

Train yourself to take a break when you are in the middle of a frantic day. Your nerves, brain, and muscles will thank you for it. Taking yourself out of a stressful situation or environment—even if it is just for five minutes—gives you the chance to get yourself back together again. It will clear your head and allow you to see the situation from a distance. Instead of lighting a cigarette and sipping coffee, try walking around and stretching your limbs, while taking some deep, relaxing breaths. Don't allow your thoughts to dwell on the issue you are working on, but keep yourself anchored in the present and focused on your body.

one thing 1 at a time

Trying to do several things at the same time is one of the most energy-wasting habits you can adopt. In fact, the inability to see one thing through to the end before focusing on another task is often seen as a tell-tale sign of stress. When you focus your whole attention on one task only, chances are that you will do a better job and finish it more quickly and without mistakes. If your work involves running a busy household or doing manual work, it can actually be downright dangerous to juggle too many things at the same time. Therefore try and "live in the moment." You will be happier and more productive for it.

people who keep stiff upper lips find that it's damn hard to smile.

Judith Guest

quote:

In every person's life there are stressful situations which cannot be avoided totally. Let's say the thought of your partner's family descending on you every Sunday already sends your stress levels soaring. One possible solution would be to invite them for afternoon tea or a light meal instead of lunch. That way you can shorten the time you have to spend together without upsetting anyone. This tactic can be applied to most situations that you find annoying or stressful. It also helps to remember it is far more important—for yourself and everyone else concerned—to be relaxed and happy than to struggle with misunderstood martyrdom.

make time for the things you want to do

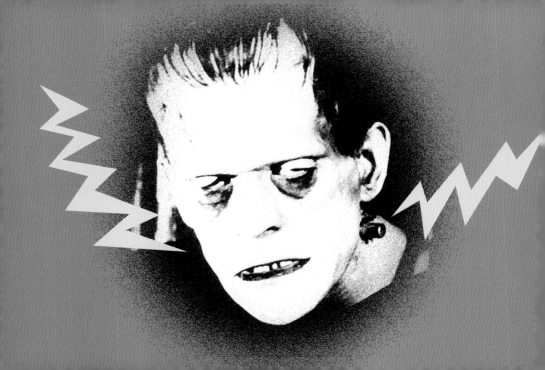

recharge your batteries

Make a point of giving yourself time on a regular basis to do the things which are important for your relaxation and happiness. Whether it is spending some time listening to your favorite music or going for a swim, choose something just for your needs. Maybe, for example, you've always wanted to try yoga, or join an art class, go ice skating, or book a relaxing aromatherapy massage. Whatever you choose, make sure you fit it into your schedule as an important time for recharging your batteries.

*turn your face
to the sun and the
shadows fall
behind you.*

Maori proverb

quote:

simulate a smile

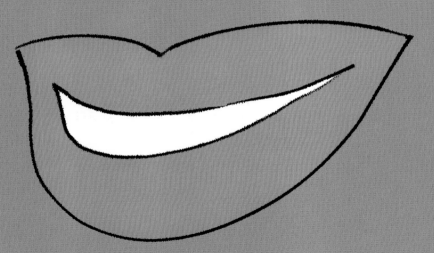

he who smiles
rather than
rages is always
the stronger.

Japanese proverb

practice random
acts of kindness
and senseless
acts of beauty

The words say it all! Being kind without a reason or the expectation of a reward is one of the most liberating things we can do. It instantly makes us feel good because it reminds us there is more to a human being than just what meets the eye. Try practicing random acts of kindness and beauty like the woman who paid the toll fee for the next ten cars behind her driving across the Golden Gate Bridge. Imagine her feelings of joy and connectedness when she saw the smiles and gestures of thank you from the drivers of these cars!

*to be for one day
entirely at leisure is
to be for one day
an immortal.*

Chinese proverb

smoothing the way: massage

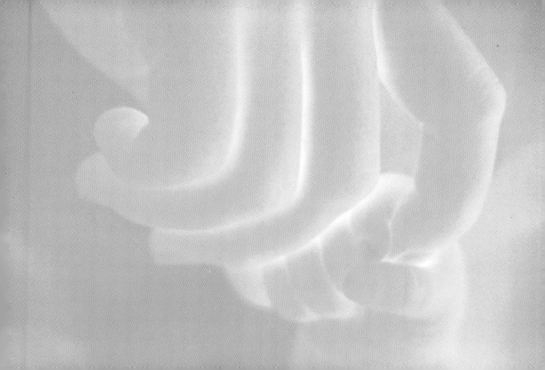

touch

communicates a
sense of peace
and connects us
with our inner selves

ouch is an instinctive response to comfort and soothe. Massage encourages the release of endorphins, the body's natural painkiller, which creates a sense of well-being. Massage improves circulation and encourages the muscles to relax, relieving tension and releasing toxins. Follow a few basic rules to give a calming massage. Find a comfortable, warm place, and cover the parts of the body you are not working on. The secret of a good massage is rhythm; keep your hands moving all the time, but do not rush. Never do anything painful and don't massage directly over the spine. Avoid hard chopping motions unless you have had some training.

Start and end your massage with effleurage, a soothing rhythmic stroke which relaxes the body. It makes a link between you and your partner and tells you how much pressure they like. The hands should glide up the body toward the heart in a stroking motion, moving together or following one another in gentle movements.

A kneading motion is a deep technique which works into the center of the muscle to ease out tightness, tension, and toxins. Go carefully to avoid causing pain. Use the "V" between your thumb and first finger to lift the muscle away from the bone and then compress it by pulling the muscles with the fingers back toward the thumb in a kneading motion. Use the thumbs to apply gentle pressure to the small muscles in the hands and feet, or very tight muscles, but never cause pain and never apply pressure on a bone or a joint.

the basic techniques of massage

massage the back to relax the whole body

Oil your hands, and make long, light sweeping movements up the back with your palms, feeling tension with your fingertips. Move in slow, sweeping half circles, up to the shoulders, down the sides, and back to the waist. Next diagonally slide your hands from hip to torso on each side of the spine.

With one hand on each side of the spine, use the pads of your thumbs to make small circular motions from the top of the back to the waist, avoiding the spine. Place your index and third finger each side of the spine and repeatedly run your hands, one after the other, down the length of the back. Finally brush the whole back with light, feathery movements. Make sure you are sometimes the recipient of this soothing massage!

quote:

if you don't relax, I'll break my fingers;
look at this—the only man in the world
with clenched hair.

Neil Simon, *The Odd Couple*

Exchange this massage with a partner for a deeply relaxing experience. Make your partner warm and comfortable, and apply talcum powder to their foot. Lightly stroke the foot between your palms, with one hand above and one below. Using the pads of your thumbs, gently knead under the arch. Press your knuckles into the sole of the foot while turning your wrist as far as it will go. Place the thumbs on the ball of the foot and apply deep, slow, circular pressures. Gently pull each toe with the finger and thumb of one hand. Circle the ankle with the fingers, press, and hold for four seconds. Then wring the ankle like delicate laundry. Finally, place one hand above and one below the foot and stroke it repeatedly between the palms from heel to toes.

a soothing foot massage: the ultimate luxury

reward and pamper
your hard-working hands with a
blissful massage

ently lift your partner's hand and support it in your hand. Keeping an even rhythm and pressure, slowly stroke up the center of the back of the hand with both thumbs. Supporting with one hand, use the thumb of the other to follow the gaps between each finger. Trace the spaces between the bones up the back of their hand. Now turn the hand palm up and rest their hand in yours. With the pads of your thumbs, make deep, circular movements in one spot in the palm. Repeat all over the palm. Then soothe the palm by making a fist and stroking the hand from fingertip to wrist. Make a series of little squeezes along the length of each finger, one after another. Finally, repeat the calming stroking moves you started with.

quick ways

to relieve stress at

work

signs of **stress** at work

Sleeplessness, irritability, anger, losing your appetite or starting to overeat, constant tiredness, inexplicable aches and pains, and no enthusiasm for your activities are all signs you may be under too much stress at work. If you have more than three symptoms you need to make sure you counteract these influences with stress-reducing activites such as meditation, relaxation techniques, and a good diet.

I am free to be joyous.

Louise Hay

Shoulders are meant to carry joy not burdens, but how many of us get headaches from tight shoulders? In the office environment tension is built up in the upper body because the majority of our activity is mental and the physical body only stays active within a restricted set of margins. Yet releasing the tension out of the upper body and shoulders is easy. Lift your shoulders up and then allow them to drop and rotate them around a horizontal axis. Then lift the shoulders up again while you take a deep breath in. On the out breath, feel them totally relax, while affirming to yourself "I am free to be joyous."

shrug shoulders

marble energizer

Put some marbles in a large plastic bowl and roll them under your foot while sitting down. This simple exercise acts like a fast massage, and stimulates the reflex points on the soles of the feet and effectively relaxes and energizes the whole body. Then repeat with the other foot. A similar effect can be achieved by exercising with a footsie roller, available from beauty shops.

take a
breather

the lungs rule qi.

Su Wen

I n Chinese medicine, the lungs are the upper source of energy for all the body's functions. If you were to spread the lungs out, the surface area would equal that of a tennis court. In most activities we use between a half and two-thirds of the lungs' capacity. Exercises that open and encourage the use of the lungs are invaluable for relaxation. Take a short walk, focus on relaxing your limbs by swinging them freely with a soft, even rhythm, let go of your thoughts and feel the breath inspiring you. As you breathe out, let go of all your worries and problems. For this one moment just relax and let go. Breathe in natural surroundings, near to trees and water. They are a source of energy for the lungs.

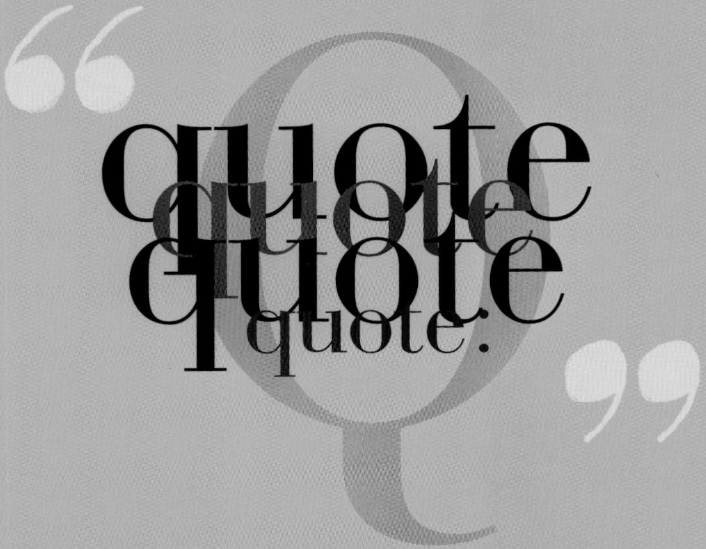
quote
quote
quote
quote:

work keeps at bay three great evils: boredom, vice, and need.

Voltaire

Plants have a unique relationship with animals and humans alike, called symbiosis. We breathe in the oxygen that is essential for our health and metabolism and as a biproduct we breathe out carbon dioxide. Plants take in carbon dioxide to produce sugars and then breathe out oxygen which for them is a biproduct of their metabolic processes. Therefore remind yourself to enjoy the company of plants, since you are exchanging something that is valuable; much to our detriment, we humans have separated ourselves from nature through ignorance. In native Nigerian medicine, however, plants are deemed to be the most intelligent creatures on the planet. Be with the plant world and relax in their presence.

me co-exist with nature

Don't try and be a superperson. There is only a certain amount you yourself can accomplish in a day, and you are certainly not the only one who can do the job well. The secret to being efficient is to know how to delegate. Therefore, if you are lucky enough to have people around you to whom you can delegate, do it! It will free you up to do what you do best.

Are you anxious about going to work, because you feel that your boss places too many demands on you? There are several tactics you can use to help you deal with this problem. Keep in mind your boss is only a human being just as you are. What makes him or her demanding are probably the pressures that he or she experiences from the people who are his or her superiors.

Also, you can influence the atmosphere in your workplace by spreading a feeling of calm and goodwill. If you don't allow yourself to get uptight, this mental attitude will eventually influence everyone around you, including your boss!

Above all, take it lightly! Nothing can really affect you in a bad way, unless you allow it to. Remember: you are the only one in control of your thoughts!

how to
deal with a
demanding
boss

lunchtime
workouts

It is all too easy to slip off to the canteen or bar and land up doing what you have been doing all morning: sitting down, talking, and, of course, eating. But this time can be used in a productive way. It is a wonderful challenge to build up to swimming a mile in half an hour and then eating lunch. Take a brisk walk through the local park and eat your sandwiches in the company of squirrels. Or go to the gym and work out, followed by a shower and a healthy salad. It is up to you to explore the options so you can make the most of your spare time in fulfilling your needs. By releasing your pent-up energy in a safe way, you will be a more pleasant person to live and work with.

When people get anxious or stressed, their breathing changes. Instead of taking in full, slow breaths, their breathing pattern becomes shallow and rapid, and their speech becomes fast and powerless. Therefore, it makes sense to concentrate on your breath when you feel yourself starting to get wound up and tense. Conscious deep breathing will allow you to draw more oxygen into your lungs while helping you to relax and let go on the emotional and physical level. Whereas shallow breathing only involves the upper third of the lungs, deep, full breaths make use of the lungs' total capacity and help to expel any accumulated stale air. The effects of deep breathing can be observed almost immediately. You'll feel more relaxed, calm, and clearer in your mind in no time at all.

take a **deep** breath

I have a new philosophy: I'm only going to dread one day at a time.

Charles Schulz, *Peanuts*

" quote:

burn a

mood

enhancing

oil

In Japan big companies have started to blow essential lemon or grapefruit oils through their air-conditioning systems. The managers know productivity will be enhanced if they help their staff to keep a clear head and a fresh mind throughout a busy day.

Lemon and grapefruit are mood-enhancing oils, whereas basil and rosemary help to clear a foggy mind and induce better concentration. Essential oils work well in synergy—that means using two or three different oils together, which will increase their positive effect. So, for example, using a mixture of grapefruit and rosemary in a little diffuser or vaporizer will definitely help make your day more pleasant.

Our body mass is made up of 70 percent water. Water is the basis of life on this planet. Without water we would be unable to survive. Yet most people do not realize the importance of drinking adequate amounts of water every day. Coffee, tea, or other beverages like juices and carbonated drinks are no substitute for clear, pure H_2O. Physicians usually recommend eight glasses of water a day, although some people find they need more to keep in peak condition. Water cleanses the system, clears constipation, alleviates headaches, and keeps the aging process at bay. But most importantly it helps you to stay calm and relaxed. Drinking a few glasses of pure water at room temperature, or slightly cooler, will work wonders as an immediate stress-buster.

wonderful water

refocus your eyes

the pure qi or energy of all the organs pours through the eyes.

Chinese medicine

I t is all too easy to strain the eyes by reading with insufficient light or letting them get lazy by wearing glasses when they are unnecessary, or on the other hand not wearing glasses when they are definitely needed. When the eyes get tired, rest them by refocusing them on near and far objects and then rotate the eyeball around in its socket. Let the eyes go into and then out of focus, as if you are looking at everything in a haze. Friction rub the heels of the hands together until they are warm and on the out breath gently place one onto each eye socket. Remember the old saying "the eyes are the windows of the soul," care for them as you would your most precious possession.

freedom is a word I rarely use.

Donovan, *Colors*

Saying "no" is not an aggressive statement. Learning to say "no" to others when appropriate and saying "yes" to yourself are positive, stress-reducing habits. Unlearning the negative conditioning of always seeking approval by wanting to please others is taking a huge step in personal freedom. By saying "no" when you need to say it gives you more time for you. It is an excellent tool for disarming the person who wants to steam roller you into their belief and then leave you feeling as if they have taken your power away. Saying "no" is the number one step in becoming an assertive communicator and, besides, saying "no" can be fun.

nein

no

nicht

iie

non

nie

nein

nie

hayır

shi

no

ohi

iie

nada

ni

la

There is something wonderfully relaxing about day dreaming. If you feel totally tense and overworked, why not start to plan your next vacation? Get some brochures from your travel agent and start thinking about where you would like to go to. If you have already made your vacation plans, remind yourself once in a while of the pleasures you are looking forward to by browsing through your brochures. Whether it is a few days by the sea or skiing in the mountains, allow your imagination to transport you to that location right now and enjoy the feeling of relaxation and positive excitement that comes over you!

don't just do something, stand there!

(A recovering workaholic)

When you find yourself stuck in a rut and your stress levels are soaring sky high, break the pattern by doing something different. Concentrate on lifting your cup with the other hand, sit in a different chair, which you would not normally sit in, put the phone to the ear you don't normally use. Doing things differently makes us think about our actions and puts us in touch with the present. Or do nothing at all! Sometimes just switching off and doing nothing is the best remedy for a stressed-out mind.

be
different

Sometimes the only way to get yourself together again may be to take a day off work. Taking a sick day once in a while is a valid way to give yourself the space and time to avoid a total burn-out. If you feel yourself on the downward spiral of stress overload, your body will be mobilizing all its energies to cope with the situation. Because your system will become depleted this can lead to depression and physical illness. So taking a day off in time will recharge your batteries and put you into a more positive frame of mind before your body starts to give you more serious warning signs. Both you and your company will benefit from it.

Laughter researcher Dr Fry describes laughter as a "whole body experience" which affects all systems of the body. As you begin to laugh your body is exercised; indeed one to two hundred good belly laughs a day is apparently equivalent to 10 minutes rowing or jogging. This "internal massage" has the added benefit of leaving you with soothed, relaxed muscles and a warm afterglow. Laughter releases catecholamines into the bloodstream, which reduce inflammation, enhance the blood flow, and speed the healing process. Laughter is indeed the best medicine.

laughter is like

the human body

wagging its tail

regain
your calm
at work
with on-site
massage

Persuade your company to employ a masseuse one morning a week. They can gently ease tired and tense neck, shoulder, and back muscles without you leaving the office. They will either bring a special chair with them, or you can sit supported on a table, cushioned by pillows. This type of massage is performed clothed, and without the use of oils. Studies show people work more effectively after massage and it can reduce absenteeism.

Sink into a gloriously relaxing and sensuous bath after work and let your worries and cares fade away while you take time for you. Add 3 drops cedarwood, 2 drops frankincense oil, and 2 drops lime oil for a deliciously stimulating combination of woody, spicy, and citrus smells to relieve stress and tone up both your body and your mind.

blissful
bathing

share it with a

with a

friend

the miracle
of touch

Touch is one of the oldest healing methods we know, and it can work wonders for your sense of well-being. Touch is vital for all age groups—without it we soon feel isolated and depressed. It is crucial to hug and cuddle your children, but it is just as important that you get enough physical affection and contact yourself. Make a point of making time for cuddles with your partner and your children, and you will be surprised at the level of comfort and happiness that comes from it.

*I no doubt deserved
my enemies, but I don't
believe I deserved
my friends.*

Walt Whitman

"quote:"

dinner for **2**

hen we are stuck in a rut, doing something that is not part of our normal routine can help break the vicious cycle. So next time you feel stressed and overwhelmed, make a date with your best friend or your partner to go out for the evening and enjoy a wonderful meal together. Try out different cuisine, forget about counting calories, maybe have an expensive bottle of wine instead of settling for the cheaper one. However, make sure you leave your problems at home—carrying your backpack of "worry bricks" with you will definitely defeat the object of the exercise!

If you are really upset and don't know where to turn, there is nothing better than having a good friend providing the proverbial shoulder to cry on. Problems have a way of becoming clearer and easier to deal with as soon as they are voiced, whereas keeping your troubles to yourself can send you into anxiety and depression. Let it all out, and you may feel ready to move on.

a
shoulder
to
cry
on

quote:

of all the gifts that a wide providence grants us to make life full and happy, friendship is the most beautiful.

Epicurus

If you feel that you don't have anyone whom you can really trust, just imagine yourself a perfect friend. Sit in a comfy chair in a quiet room, close your eyes and create as vivid a picture of this person in your mind as you can. Then allow yourself to hand your problem over to that imaginary friend. Stay with your eyes closed and listen for any answers or solutions that may form in your mind. This can be a very powerful practice as it allows you to tap into a level of energy that is beyond what we normally perceive with our five senses.

create your perfect

companion

a burden shared is a burden halved

Sometimes, on top of our workload at the office, we are also faced with extra jobs and obligations to be dealt with at home. If you feel these extra tasks will just push you to the end of your tether, try to negotiate a deal with a friend. Since everyone experiences those times of added stress, it really does make sense to help each other out in times of need. Perhaps, for example, your friend can look after your children for the night when you know you'll have to work late, and you could look after hers when she is going for that job interview and needs to function and look her best.

*the proper office of a friend
is to side with you when you are in the
wrong; nearly anybody will side with
you when you are in the right.*

Mark Twain

quote:

Feet are incredibly rewarding recipients of massage and stroking. Usually we don't pay enough attention to our feet and yet they have to carry us around all day. Often people are apprehensive about having their feet touched because they expect a tickling sensation. But as long as the strokes are not applied too lightly and gingerly and you work in a steady and calm rhythm, massaging each other's feet can induce wonderful feelings of relaxation and well-being. Follow your inner feeling about what kind of touch is right for your partner, and allow yourself to be totally present in the moment. You may find giving a massage in this frame of mind will take you out of your preoccupation with your own problems and leave you with a wonderful feeling of warmth and comfort.

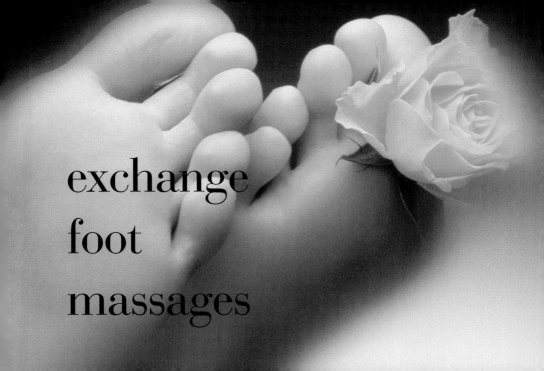

exchange
foot
massages

stress-free travel

be realistic

L et's face it—traveling is usually stressful. There is all the packing and organizing beforehand, so the last thing you want to do is to have to rush or wreck your nerves over being late. Whether it is about being at the airport or train station in time, or driving to a meeting in your own car, make sure you leave yourself plenty of time to get there. It may only be half an hour from your home to the airport under optimum conditions, but a few red traffic lights or a broken-down truck can turn the easy drive into a desperate dash to catch that plane, if you haven't allowed extra time.

leave plenty of time

Make your journey as pleasant for yourself as you can. If you know you are going to be in the car for a long period of time, make sure you have some tapes with your favorite music with you. Allow yourself the luxury of singing to the music at the top of your voice, releasing all the tension that has accumulated.

Surely you have noticed how much relief you can get from spilling all your troubles and worries out in front of a trusted friend. The next time you are stuck in a traffic jam, you could just pick up your cell phone and give your friend a call. You might as well make the most of the delay by sharing your experience. Also, if you are generally pressed for time which makes it difficult for you to keep in touch, this is a good opportunity to catch up on the latest news from your friends. So, the next time you are stuck in traffic, see it as a blessing in disguise which gives you the time to re-enforce your circle of friends.

record your thoughts

Because the best ideas often come in the car, it makes sense to have a portable tape recorder with you to use instead of a notebook to record your thoughts. Dictating all your wonderful ideas onto it or dictating letters makes great use of your time and makes sure that you don't feel you have wasted precious hours. Alternatively, have some learning or self-improvement tapes handy, and make the best of your time.

eureka!

time to solve problems

Traveling can be a wonderful time to deal with things you have postponed because of a lack of time. While your brain switches to autopilot driving the car, your creative mind can mull over problems and issues that may have bothered you for quite a while. Whether it is planning a family get-together, dealing with a difficult task at work, or figuring out how to handle your child's stressed-out teacher, the best solutions can often be found in the solitude of a long journey.

I am righteously indignant;
you are annoyed; he is making a fuss
about nothing.

Competition, *New Statesman*

On long journeys, especially when you are stuck in traffic in your car, it is important to keep muscle tension at bay. Remind yourself to let your hands rest lightly instead of clutching the steering wheel, and sit as straight, yet as relaxed, as you can. Whenever possible, get out of the car and loosen your limbs, neck, and shoulders. It is important to take frequent breaks to stay concentrated and alert when you are driving. As the old saying goes: "Rather be late than the late."

keep mobile

energy
in motion

moving meditation: the joy of tai chi and chi gong

that which shrinks must first expand.

Lao Tsu

Tai chi and chi gong are forms of exercise which have been used in the Orient for thousands of years to promote spiritual, emotional, and physical well-being. They teach techniques of standing and moving in set patterns to exercise the body, mind, and spirit in pure relaxation and balance. The Four Seasons movement described on the following pages involves wonderful, flowing movements while holding a visual pattern of each season in your mind. It is important to hold each seasonal position for 3–5 minutes initially. After that, gradually allow the positions to flow into each other to become one slow and elegant movement.

Stand with your feet parallel and a shoulder's width apart, knees unlocked, and with your back straight. Relax everything above the waist and focus your attention on a point just below your navel. Hold your hand out in front of your chest, fingers separated like the branches of a tree. While holding this position, imagine being filled with the energy and vitality of spring.

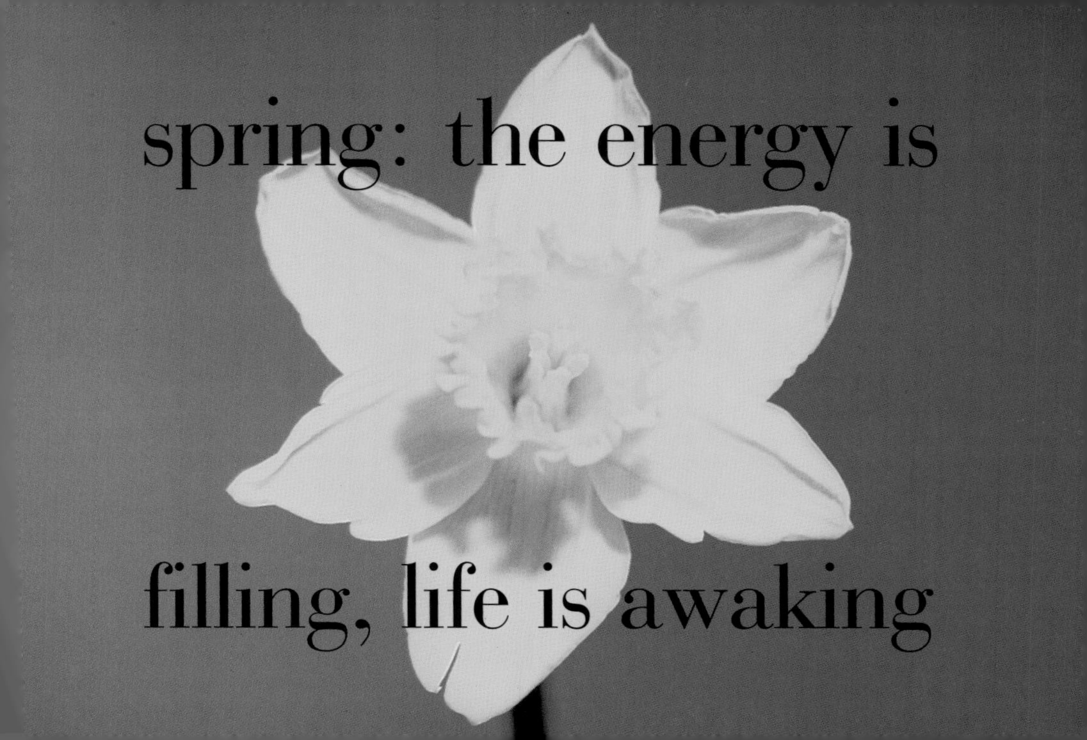

spring: the energy is

filling, life is awaking

renew thyself
completely each day;
do it again,
and again,
forever again.

Chinese inscription

quote:

summer: the energy

I magine standing in the warmth of a sunny midsummer's day. Remaining in the basic standing position, allow your arms to reach up toward an imaginary sun, spreading out wide without overstretching. Your feet might want to turn slightly outward at this point. Eventually your body should take on the shape of a fluted wineglass, spilling over with the abundant energy of summer.

is full and abundant

fall: in the fullness of harvest the energy is starting to turn inward till in the basic standing position, allow your feet to return to parallel, while you lower your arms to your side, holding them slightly away from your body. Turn your palms toward the ground as if resting on a giant fruit. Allow all your tension to drop as gently as leaves falling off a tree.

winter: the energy is

Imagine yourself in the stillness of a dark winter's night, curled up and secure. From the position of fall allow your toes to turn in towards each other, as your body contracts and folds up into a foetal position, whilst your breathing is focused on emptying. In this position wait for the natural feeling of rising into spring.

concentrated in the seed

midday
pick-me-ups

Usually our bodies give us very clear messages if we take the time to listen. Our concentration and effectiveness very much depend on how we respond to those inner messages. Sometimes you might start feeling tired in the middle of the day. Instead of trying to ignore the feeling, nibble on a piece of fruit to see if low blood sugar levels are the cause for your tiredness. Sometimes it helps just to close your eyes and switch off for a few moments. At other times your body will want you to get up and move around to get your energy revitalized. In any case, it is important to follow through on the messages your body gives to you. Your rewards will be renewed energy and the ability to cope better with the rest of the day.

body clock messages

lunch like a king: eggplant, artichoke, and tomato phyllo tart

5 tablespoons olive oil

$\frac{1}{2}$ teaspoon ground red chili

four 13- x 13-inch sheets phyllo or strudel dough

1 eggplant, weighing about 12 ounces, sliced

3 oil-cured bottled or canned artichokes, quartered lengthwise

3 large garlic cloves, unpeeled

4 plum tomatoes

salt and freshly ground black pepper

2 ounces dry goat cheese and 3 ounces mozzarella cheese, both sliced

2 teaspoons chopped fresh thyme

ombine the oil with the chili and use to brush a 1½-inch deep, 9-inch, loose-bottomed tart pan. Cover the dough with a damp kitchen towel. Using one sheet at a time, dab one side with the chili oil and layer in the pan, covering the bottom and pressing the dough up the sides; fold the edges over before adding the next sheet. Bake in a heated oven at 400° for 12 to 15 minutes, until golden. Brush the eggplant slices with the chili oil and place on a baking tray with the artichokes and garlic cloves. Bake for 20 minutes at 400°. Skin and mash the garlic. Skin, seed, and slice the tomatoes; pat dry. Smear the pastry case with the garlic. Arrange the eggplant, artichoke and tomato, on top and season with salt and pepper. Top with the cheeses and sprinkle with thyme. Bake for 15 to 20 minutes, until the cheese melts.

Have you ever thought about allowing yourself the luxury of a lunchtime nap? Maybe you have had a late night the evening before and your concentration and energy are really low. Or maybe you have expended all your energy already throughout the morning because it has been one of those ultrahectic days. If you feel like it, allow yourself a little cat nap instead of pushing yourself even harder. You may be surprised how much refreshment and calmness can come from a few minutes of snoozing—even if it is only at your desk.

take a nap

take a walk in the park

Walking is a wonderful way of exercising without exhausting yourself. If you have the chance to get out into a nearby park during your lunch break, a brisk walk, while swinging your arms and breathing deeply will quickly replenish your depleted energies and leave you fresh and alert. Don't be put off by a little rain—the cleansing quality of the water will be an additional bonus to your activity. You'll return to your office with rosy cheeks and sparkling eyes, all ready to tackle whatever the afternoon may bring.

poem

I refuse to be intimidated by
reality anymore.
After all, what is reality anyway?
Nothin' but a collective hunch . . .
I made some studies, and
reality is the leading cause of stress
amongst those in
touch with it. I can take it in small
doses, but as a lifestyle
I found it too confining.

Jane Wagner

Research proves what many cultures have long known: yogurt is genuinely health promoting. It is believed to boost the immune system and discourage the proliferation of harmful bacteria in the gut. Dried apricots and bananas are packed with energy-giving carbohydrates. Keep apricot purée in the refrigerator ready for the blender to treat yourself to this quick, natural pick-me-up.

Boil $\frac{1}{4}$ cup dried apricots, preferably unsulfured, in $\frac{3}{4}$ cup water until soft. Tip water and apricots into a blender and puree until smooth and leave to cool. Add one sliced banana, $\frac{2}{3}$ cup plain yoghurt, and three tablespoons orange juice and blend. Pour into a tumbler and sprinkle with toasted flaked almonds and a twist of orange.

yogurt, banana, and dried
apricot shake yoghurt

hug a tree

the standing people provide oxygen for the rest of the children of the earth.

Jamie Sams

The Cherokees teach that trees are the givers that constantly provide for the needs of others. At the first sign of an illness the Cherokees began an activity they called "sitting in the lap of mother." This meant going into the forest and sitting with their backs against a strong, mature tree, soaking up the energy and healing this wonderful being would provide.

In our time we seem to have forgotten about the power of nature to heal and replenish our bodies and minds. Yet studies on patient recuperation in hospitals have shown that those patients with a view of trees through their hospital window recover much quicker than those who are separated from nature. So next time you feel out of balance, try and make friends with a tree.

The ancient sages of China did not see treating sick people as their main job. They concentrated on instructing those who were not ill. Constant tension and tightness, if untreated, can lead to serious problems in the human body. Acupressure is an age-old therapy of applying pressure to certain points on the energetic pathways throughout the body known as energy meridians. You can benefit from this by using the following acupressure points to release the tension in your neck and shoulders, clear a lingering headache, and induce the most remarkable feeling of calm.

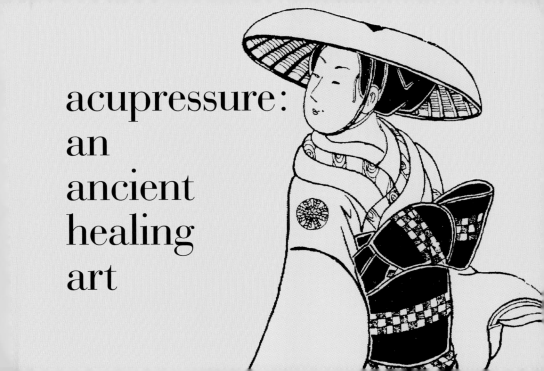

acupressure: an ancient healing art

getting to the point

O n the back of your head feel for the area where the skull joins the neck. Place both your thumbs there and slowly slide them out toward the ears. You will come to a deep hollow, called "Feng Chi" in Chinese medicine. Massage this area with your thumbs and apply an upward pressure on both sides until you feel a dull ache. Keep the pressure on for about thirty seconds and then slowly release. Repeat this procedure several times until you feel your muscles start to relax.

find your relax

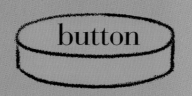
button

Draw an imaginary line over the top of your head connecting your ears. Where this line meets the vertical axis going through your body, you find another highly effective acupressure point called "Bai Hui." While supporting the back of your head with one hand, use the index finger of your other hand to apply pressure and massage this point slowly in a clockwise direction. Again, you may find this spot is very tender, especially if you are tense. Keep massaging the area for as long as feels comfortable, but at least for a couple of minutes to induce a feeling of deep relaxation. Then let your arms gently drop down by your side, close your eyes, and sit quietly for a little while.

Whenever you feel yourself really stuck with a problem and can't seem to find a way out, you may want to symbolically remove your blinkers and see if your creative subconscious can come up with a new solution. There are always answers to our problems, waiting to be discovered. The important thing is to learn how to switch off our logical mind and allow our intuition to guide us. This wonderful "sixth sense" is far more connected to the bigger picture than your conscious mind will ever be. And the important things in life—spending time with your family, looking after your health, taking time to be kind to others—will come back into perspective, and work worries, financial problems, while important, will regain their rightful proportion.

see the
big
picture

burn an energizing aromatherapy **oil**

If you're feeling weary in the afternoon, lighten the load and energize yourself with an invigorating aromatherapy oil. Try vaporizing a combination of bay and ginger oil for a stimulating scent. This combination also makes a refreshing footbath.

It is wonderful to watch children enjoying playing with soil; we adults can forget how important it is to stay in touch with the earth. After a day of working hard with your brain, your head full of lofty ideas, it can be relaxing to ground yourself by making contact with mother earth again. Weeding, digging, preparing space and planting new plants can reconnect you with the original rhythm of life, which is reassuring, steady and strong. Problems and worries are put into perspective as you start to feel alive in your body again and energetically replenished. And enjoying the satisfaction of a beautiful, flowering or productive garden as the result of your own hard labor often provides incredibly powerful healing for your stressed body and tired mind.

the sole connection: reflexology

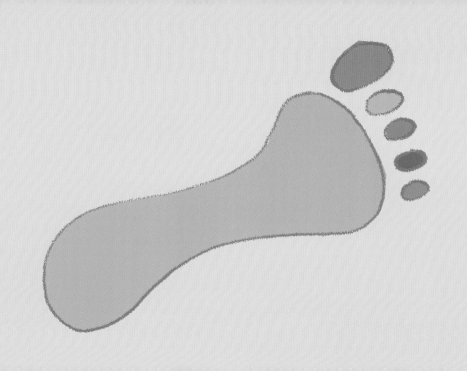

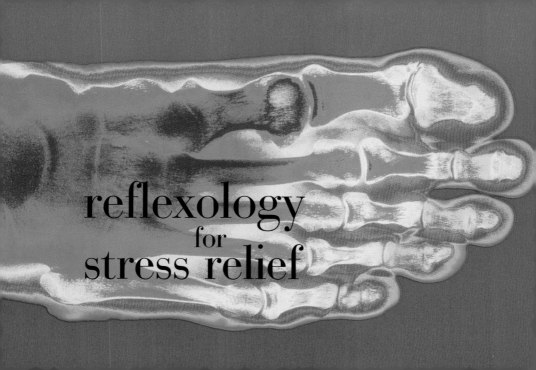

reflexology
for
stress relief

Reflexology is a gentle, natural, and safe holistic therapy available to everyone. It is particularly useful as a self-help stress reliever and the only equipment required is a pair of hands. Reflexology is based on the theory that all organs and parts of the body are represented in the foot by individual reflex points. Any congestion in the body will manifest as tenderness in the corresponding area on the foot. By working over these reflex points with gentle pressure, it is possible to restore the body's natural balance and, therefore, help to relieve stress. You can exchange treatments with a friend, or give yourself a treatment by making yourself comfortable in a chair and resting the foot you are working on the opposite knee.

The basic technique for reflexology is the application of gentle pressure, using the top part of your thumb, between the nail and the pad of the thumb. You need to apply firm but gentle pressure: do not use a rubbing action. There is no need to use a carrier oil as this will cause the fingers to slip over reflexes; it is preferable to use talcum powder. Always massage both feet, one after the other. To help relaxation before you begin, and to increase blood flow to the area, place both hands each side of the right foot and briskly rub each side of the ankle joint to "wobble" the foot from side to side. Then repeat on the left foot.

reflexology
techniques

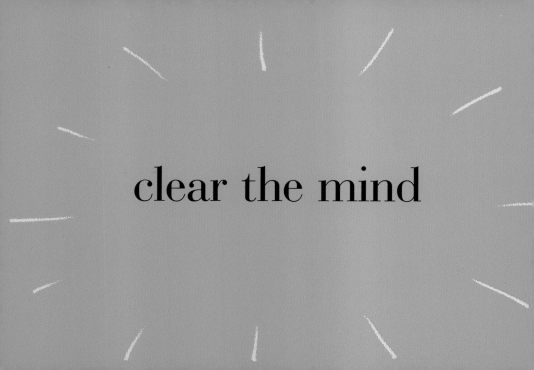

clear the mind

R educe tension with reflexology and clear the mind. Support the right foot with your left hand by placing the fingers over the back of the foot and the thumb across the ball of the foot. Gently press the thumb of your right hand into the center of the pad of the big toe and release. Moving in a clockwise direction, work all over the pad of the toe.

To reduce tension in the neck, support the right foot with your left hand by placing the fingers over the back of the foot and the thumb across the ball of the foot. Starting from the outside of the toe, press along the neck of the toe using firm, gentle pressure. Press, release, and move on, working up the inside of the toe to the tip. Repeat with the remaining toes.

S upport the top of the foot with your left hand and, using the top of your thumb, start at the inside heel and work slowly up the arch in small steps. Press, release, and move on. Imagine a caterpillar walking! Continue to the big toe and then work back down using the left hand, (right hand supporting foot).

To slow your breathing, support the back of the foot with your left hand. Form a fist with your right hand and gently push into the ball of the foot. Then pull the toes downward in a wavelike action. Repeat several times. Finish by stroking the foot with both hands, left hand on the top, right hand underneath, from the toes to the ankle.

do the caterpillar walk

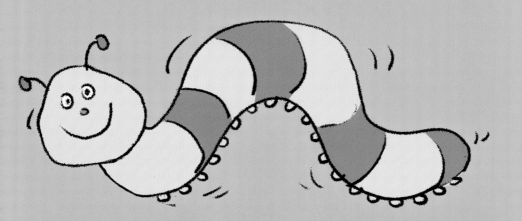

reflexology to relieve tired eyes

Support the right foot with your left hand and press the pad of the right thumb into the skin directly below the base of the second toe. Keep the thumb bent to make sure the tip of the thumb pad presses into the correct area. Continue with a caterpillar-crawl action under all the other toes to the little toe. Change hands and work back up to the second toe using the left hand. Finish your sequence by supporting the right foot with your left hand and using the right thumb to caterpillar walk across the heel approximately two finger-widths from its bottom. Work from right to left and then change hands and work back, left to right.

relax
at home

nergize your home with houseplants, which will help absorb common toxic substances in your home. Azaleas, rubber plants, poinsettias, and bamboo palms all remove formaldehyde from the air. Other plants remove acetone, benzene, methanol, and other harmful chemicals. Plants also give off oxygen which will enhance the atmosphere. So fill your house with plants for a healthier home!

plant
magic

Evaluate the atmosphere of your home environment and take some simple, positive steps to reduce the effect of everyday pollutants and stressors that may affect your well-being. Choose natural wood furniture which has been sealed with a natural varnish. Choose wool, cotton, or natural-fiber rugs, rather than wall-to-wall, synthetic carpets. Natural linoleum, ceramic, or cork are healthy floor coverings. Use natural paints rather than ones based on petroleum products. Follow these steps and your home will be a healthier place for you and your family.

Orange essential oil has a cheering, refreshing scent which revives the spirits. Make a wood-shaving, chili, and orange potpourri to energize your living room. Cut patterns in an organic or unwaxed orange and leave in a well-ventilated place to dry slowly and naturally. Mix together in a bowl with wood shavings and dried chilies, and add a few drops rosemary, orange, and coriander oil for a refreshing, spicy scent.

reviving the spirits

Turn off the lights and light your room simply with candles to relax your eyes and your spirits. Take the space to listen to some tranquil music or talk to your partner in this peaceful atmosphere. Or simply sit and enjoy the luxury of a quiet time just for you.

create
ₐcandlelit
place ₒf
peace

Research in retirement homes has shown old people who have a pet live longer, are less depressed and anxious and recover better from minor illnesses than those who don't. This is not surprising though, when you think about it. Pets hardly make any demands on us—they only need their daily food and, in the case of dogs, a little exercise (which is just as necessary for the owner as it is for the dog). They are affectionate, faithful, and forgiving to the extreme. And they provide us with the opportunity for cuddles and play, which are often lacking in our everyday lives. So congratulations to you, if you are already the proud owner of a pet. Enjoy it! And for those of you who are not, there are rescue homes filled to the brim with animals waiting for someone to love!

invest in

If you can't cope with the thought of getting a pet for yourself, how about investing in a tank with tropical fish? Some people love to sit in front of their aquarium for hours on end to watch the colorful display. Fish move slowly and breathe slowly. Sometimes they even remain still for a while, just breathing. Maybe we all can learn a lot from fish watching!

tropical fish

If you like natural sounds, how about buying a set of wind chimes for your garden? Sometimes it is lovely to have one set that produces high, ethereal sounds, and another one which has got a deep, earthy quality to it. Then lie down in the grass and allow yourself to be showered with the beautiful, unpredictable music produced by a gentle evening breeze.

heavenly
music

quote:

dolce far niente!
it is sweet doing nothing!

After having spent a whole day at the office working mainly with your head, it is lovely to use your creativity and your hands to produce something satisfying for your senses. Maybe you have always wanted to bake your own bread, or there is a recipe for Aunt Mary's wonderful cookies you have never tried out yourself. A lovely feeling of pleasure and satisfaction comes with a slice of delicious, fresh cake and a cup of tea while the smell of spices and baking lingers in the air.

be
creative
in the
kitchen

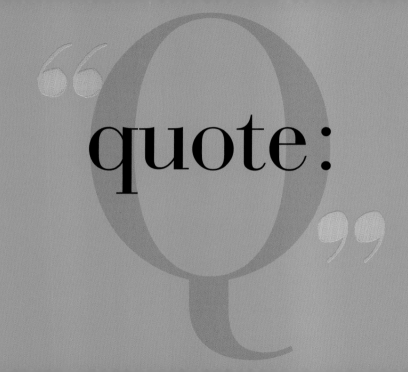

quote:

*never put off till tomorrow what you
can do the day after tomorrow.*

Mark Twain

1 cup trimmed snow peas

3 tablespoons shelled pistachio nuts

1 large ripe papaya, peeled, seeded and sliced

lime juice

1 head butterhead lettuce, such as Bibb

1 kiwifruit, peeled and thinly sliced crosswise

1 tablespoon chopped fresh mint

For the dressing:

1 tablespoon lime juice

salt

freshly ground black pepper

3 tablespoons grapeseed oil

3 tablespoons walnut or almond oil

papaya and

T his vitamin-packed, colorful salad has a tangy dressing. Like all orange-fleshed fruit, papaya is an excellent source of betacarotene. It is also rich in enzymes that aid digestion.

Plunge the snow peas into boiling water for 30 seconds. Drain immediately and leave to cool. Cover the pistachios with boiling water, leave for 5 minutes, drain, and slip off their skins. Combine the dressing ingredients. Sprinkle the papaya with lime juice. Arrange the lettuce on four plates, arrange the papaya, kiwi, and snow peas on top. Sprinkle with mint and coat with dressing.

snow pea salad

Have you ever stood by a waterfall and felt totally refreshed and revitalized by the coolness and clarity of the air around it? An ionizer can have the same effect on you. It produces the negatively charged ions which are responsible for the sparkling, refreshing atmosphere by a waterfall. Ionizers cleanse the air and allow you to breathe better, but above all they can induce that state of well-being that equals the experience by the waterfall. How does it work? Negative ions stimulate the production of serotonin in your brain, a neurotransmitter that induces sleep and relaxation.

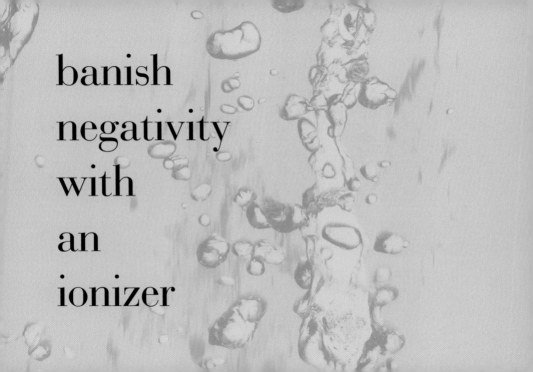

banish
negativity
with

an

ionizer

for fast-acting relief, try slowing down.

Jane Wagner

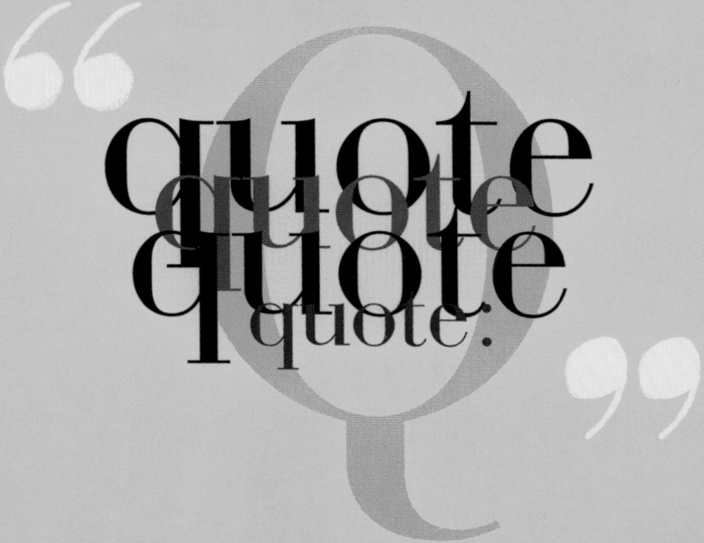
quote
quote
quote
quote:

take a sensuous

For a gloriously self-indulgent bath mixture, add three drops each of jasmine, sandalwood, and ylang ylang essential oil. This mixture has intimate, feminine overtones as well as being ideal for relieving stress. Jasmine, sometimes called the king of oils, is good for overcoming negative feelings.

aromatherapy bath

14 ounces broccoli

3 carrots

$\frac{1}{2}$ cup sugar snap peas

grated zest of 1 lemon

3 tbsps snipped garlic chives

sea salt flakes

olive oil

A quickly made dish guaranteed to keep your broccoli looking bright green instead of an unappetizing yellow. The deeper the color of the vegetables, the higher their nutritional value. The broccoli stems are too delicious to discard.

Discard the first two inches of the central broccoli stem. Cut the remaining stems into thin diagonal slices. Break the florets into small pieces. Thinly slice the carrots diagonally. Trim the sugar snap peas. Put all the vegetables into a large saucepan of boiling salted water and boil for 45 seconds, then drain immediately. Put the vegetables back in the pan with the lemon zest and garlic chives and sea salt. Drizzle with olive oil. Toss over medium heat until heated. This cooking method retains the color and the nutrients of the vegetables.

broccoli, carrot, and sugar snap peas with lemon zest and olive oil

Take your mind off your problems by indulging in an evening in front of the television. Rent a video of your favorite movie, get into some comfortable clothes, and settle down on your couch.

As you become absorbed in what is happening on the screen you inevitably forget about your worries. As your conscious mind is engaged in following the script, your subconscious has a breathing space in which to come up with solutions that are often far more creative and positive than your conscious mind could ever conjure up. At the very least you will gain some distance from whatever bothers you and end up with a better perspective.

shoot for the moon.
even if you miss,
you will land
among the stars.

Anon.

quote:

chapter 12

deep
relaxation

I n a stressful situation, breathe in through the nose for 1 or 2 seconds, pause, then breathe out through the mouth for 7 to 8 seconds. As ancient cultures have known for centuries, controlling the breath is one of the simplest and quickest ways of maintaining or regaining your composure.

a quick way to

deep calm

be a B

Psychologists divide people into type A and type B people. Type As tend to be aggressive, ambitious, irritable, hurried, demanding, dynamic, and competitive—and suffer from stress. Type Bs are relaxed, patient, receptive, caring, easy-going, careful, serene, and unambitious—and are less susceptible to stress. If you are a typical A, adopt some of B's behavior patterns to minimize the effect on your health—listen to other people; do one thing at a time; don't try to be perfect; be more compassionate and forgive other people's shortcomings; and when you start to feel angry or bossy, behave in a gentler way.

When we are under stress our bodies build up toxins. One of the most effective and simplest ways of redressing the balance is to go on a 24- or 48-hour raw-food or juice-only diet. When short of calories, the body first uses up old, diseased tissues, so this is an effective spring clean. Drink plenty of spring water to flush out the system. Take it easy, and sleep as much as you need (you may be surprised how much you want to sleep). This is a great regime for a quiet, reviving weekend.

detox your system!

pranayama:
the calming
breath

When you are stressed, your breathing becomes quicker and shallower, altering the acidity of the blood, which can lead to hyperventilation and, eventually, panic. The opposite is also true: if you are feeling uptight, you can quickly calm yourself by slowing and controlling your breathing. Practice this breathing exercise regularly to protect yourself against the effects of stress: Lie down comfortably and exhale fully through a partially open mouth for 6-8 seconds. Allow inhalation to be free; it should take 2–3 seconds. Then exhale fully again. It may take a while to learn this, but once mastered it will relieve anxiety within a couple of minutes.

inside myself is a place where I live all alone, and that's where you renew your springs that never dry up.

Pearl S. Buck

quote:

controlling
the
breath

Upper-chest breathing is both a result of anxiety and creates it. When it becomes habitual it is difficult to change without special exercises. To check if you are an upper-chest breather, find a chair with arms and sit in front of a mirror. Breathe in deeply and see if your shoulders rise. If they do, then push down with your forearms and elbows onto the arms of the chair as you inhale. This will prevent you from using the wrong muscles when breathing. Repeat ten times, exhaling for six to eight seconds, and allowing a free inhalation for two to three seconds.

meditation—the stress buster

For relaxation to work its magic on the body—to lower blood pressure, calm the nervous system, release tension in muscles, enhance immune system function, and reverse the damage done by negative stress—both the body and mind need to be still, calm, and serene. This can be achieved through meditation. The body must be calm and the breathing regular, tranquil, and easy. Meditation is a state of deep relaxation in which breathing slows, alpha and theta brainwaves increase, and the mind is calm, yet alert. Commit yourself to practicing meditation daily for six weeks and you will find it brings tranquillity and joy into your life.

too fast we live, too much are tried,
too harass'd, to attain
Wordsworth's sweet calm.

Matthew Arnold

“quote:”

a beginner's
guide to
meditation

Choose a time to meditate every day—perhaps wake up half an hour earlier than normal. Choose a place where you won't be disturbed. Sit comfortably on the floor or in a chair, with your spine straight. The key to meditation is keeping the mind focused on one subject or object. Do not become irritated if your mind wanders, simply refocus, gently, like a butterfly landing on a flower. Choose a phrase which is meaningful to you personally, such as "God is love," over and over again to blot out all other mental activity. As left side activity of the brain decreases, the intuitive, creative, right side of the brain becomes more active.

never am I less alone than when I am by myself, never am I more active than when I do nothing.

Cato

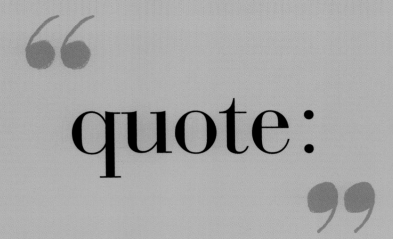
quote:

meditating

on the

breath

This is a simple meditation you can do, and you can take a few minutes to practice it anywhere. Simply sit in a comfortable position with your spine straight. Close your eyes and be aware of how your body feels. Notice the rhythm of your breathing. Feel the air as it passes through your nose and throat. Be aware of the rise and fall of every breath, letting your breathing look after itself. Count each time you inhale and exhale, up to ten, and then start at one again. If your mind wanders, simply bring your awareness back to your breath. Practicing this for five minutes increases oxygen levels in the blood, stimulates the whole body and reverses feelings of tiredness and lethargy.

It is possible to mimic the effects of a flotation tank by combining the relaxing effects of a warm bath with the semiweightless state achieved by increasing the density of water by adding Epsom salts. Simply dissove one to two pounds Epsom salts (most drug stores sell it) in a warm bath and submerge yourself in it. As you rest, wear an eye mask to block out light and so reduce outside stimulus even more.

After an Epsom-salts bath you may perspire heavily, but if you should wish to avoid sweating, shower after the bath. The best advice is to pat yourself dry and go to bed for a few hours to let the detoxification benefits of sweating take place.

flotation relaxation

“quote
quote
quote
quote:”

*turn your face
to the sun and
the shadows fall
behind you.*

Maori proverb

Autogenic training engages both the mind and the body to produce an effective form of relaxation in just 15 minutes per day. Lie comfortably on the floor with a cushion under your head and knees and focus on your right hand and silently say "my hand feels heavy." Don't worry if your attention wanders, just gently bring your focus back to your hand. Feel a pleasant sense of release in your hand. Then repeat with your left hand. Repeat this procedure with each arm and leg in turn, then on your forehead. Go back to your hand and repeat the procedure saying "my hand feels warm." Then repeat throughout the body.

mind calming
with autogenic
training

the power of the mind

Visualization is a powerful tool which you can use to relax completely. If you are sceptical about its effectiveness, try this simple test. Imagine a juicy, ripe orange. You can feel its pitted, cool skin under your fingers. You put it to your nose and it has a sharp, tangy smell. It has a thick, juicy skin and you take a knife to cut it. As you do the juice runs down the knife. You cut a segment and raise it to your mouth. You suck the tender segment. If you have imagined this sufficiently vividly, your mouth will now be filled with saliva in anticipation of eating the orange. Just thinking about a specific subject can have a powerful effect on your body. In the same way, imagining a peaceful spot can make you feel relaxed. Visualization is most powerful when all five senses are engaged, so feel, smell, see, hear, and taste the subject of your visualization.

creative goal setting

Creative imagery works best when you set goals and decide what you would really like to realize or create—such as a life with less stress. First do some relaxing breathing exercises, then create a clear mental image of the situation you would like to achieve. Always visualize the situation now (if you visualize it in the future, that's where it will remain—in the future). Bring the image to mind in meditation and at times throughout the day. Give it positive energy by making strong, positive statements.

and imagery

a visualization for tranquillity

Close your eyes and breathe in and out a few times. Imagine a bright, clean pool of water, deep in an untouched forest. Rain is drumming on the surface of the pool and you realize the shimmering of the water's face and the erratic reflection of the trees suits your mood right now. As you gaze upon the surface, it seems natural to become one with the water, to identify with the pool. But as you become one with the pool, you realize that the pool itself is deeper than the disturbance upon its surface. This realization leads you to be aware of your own untouched depths, and you are surprised to discover that those depths—peaceful and harmonious—have been there all along.

As you have been within yourself, the rain has been slacking off, and now even the pool's and your own surface have become less agitated. The rain stops altogether, and you are left serene and reflective. Enjoy, then let your eyes open. You can tape this visualization to play for yourself, possibly adding some relaxing music.

Alternate nostril breathing has been proven to balance the left and right sides of the brain, which relaxes the nervous system and calms the whole body. Sit with your back straight but relaxed. Tuck your first two fingers into the palm of your hand and place your thumb on one side of your nose and your two small fingers on the other. Close your right nostril and inhale through your left, then close your left nostril and exhale out of your right. Inhale through the right nostril, then close it and exhale through the left. Always inhale to the count of three and exhale to the count of six. Repeat this exercise for 10 rounds, then enjoy the calming effect.

breathing to
balance the •
brain

scents to soothe

smell:
the most
primal
human
sense

mell is a powerful sense which can evoke emotions, memories, and physical responses. Science is now proving what aromatherapists have known for centuries—scents can relax a tense mind and body and simply make you feel wonderful. Essential oils are derived from the flowers, stems, and leaves of plants. They are very potent and should be diluted in a carrier oil, such as peach nut or almond oil, before being used on the skin for a wonderful massage. Add five drops of pine, neroli, or jasmine to the water for an energizing, relaxing, or sensuous bath. Or use a vaporizer to fill your home or office with scent.

relaxing lavender

L avender oil comes from the flowers, leaves, and stems of the plant and is probably the best known of all the essential oils. Used in a hot bath, lavender oil helps alleviate stress and insomnia. Used in a lukewarm bath, it is refreshing and enlivening, and a massage with lavender promotes relaxation. It is safe for home use and is also excellent for treating insect bites and burns. Headaches, even migraines, respond well to lavender.

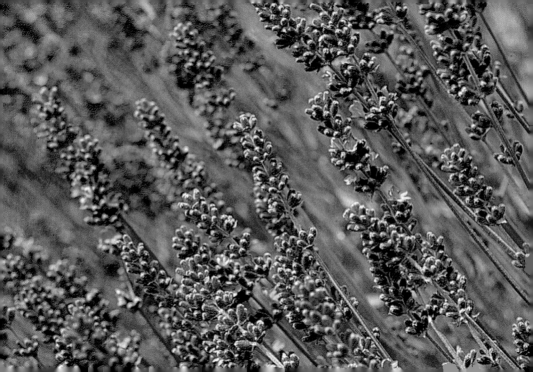

quote:

I try to have one terrific smell every day.
I like to give my nose a snack.

Jane Wagner.

This essential oil is obtained from the blossoms of the bitter orange tree and has a flowery fragrance. A natural tranquillizer, neroli is excellent for treating long-term tension and short-term stress. It is deliciously relaxing for any massage and a neroli-scented bath is wonderfully calming. If you know you are about to face a stressful situation, put a couple of drops of neroli on a tissue and inhale it from time to time.

neroli:
ₐnatural
tranquillizer

rose: remedy

This sweet, delicate essential oil comes from the petals of the flower. It is excellent for treating all kinds of depression, and can help with headaches and insomnia. It can open the heart and lift the spirits. A full body massage with rose oil is wonderfully relaxing, and a few drops in a warm bath helps with headaches, allergies, and hangovers.

for the heart

release your tension
with camomile

One of the nine sacred herbs of the Saxons, camomile is one of the gentlest and most soothing of oils. It is a natural anti-inflammatory and will help with muscle aches and emotional stresses and strains. Its sedative effects help with sleeplessness and with headaches. A very safe oil, it can help calm fractious babies, as well as fractious business people!

This essential oil has a strong, sweet aroma that is very sensuous. It is hypnotic and relaxing and is good for treating all kinds of emotional turmoil. A full-body massage with ylang ylang calms tension and counteracts negativity, and a few drops in the bath can reduce stress and alleviate fears. It is also renowned for its aphrodisiac qualities.

soothing
ylang ylang

magical color

a color meditation

I magine yourself sitting on a bench in a meadow. The air is fresh and clean after the rain and you can still see little droplets of water glistening and sparkling in the grass and on the meadow flowers. A gentle breeze is blowing through your hair and as you look up you can see a beautiful rainbow forming in the sky. It seems to arch right above you and you bathe in the vibrancy of its colors. In your mind ask quietly that the color that you need most at the moment may flow out of the rainbow and into your body, filling every cell of your being with its healing energy.

Color therapists work on the premise that each color vibrates at its own frequency, as does every organ and cell in the body. Ill health distorts these frequencies, and therapists will often use colored lights to restore the cells to balance and thus initiate healing. Many therapists work with the aura, the energy field which surrounds your body and which sensitive people can visualize as colored light, and chakras, the seven major energy centers of the body.

color therapy

The effects of color are powerful. Blind people can "see" colors through their hands, as they pick up their vibrational frequencies. We seem to absorb the energy of color through our senses and our skin. Therefore it is important we choose colors for our home we feel comfortable with. As a general guideline, use the cool, soothing colors like blue, purple, and green for bedrooms and areas where you want to relax. Kitchens and dining rooms often benefit from light orange and peach colors. If you work from home, give your office a good paint of yellow, because it enhances your ability to concentrate and stimulates mental clarity and intellectual ability. However, listen to your own feelings about what is right for you personally—some people sleep beautifully in a red bedroom!

Studies show that simply looking at red raises blood pressure, and blue effectively lowers it. Crying infants can be quieted by a blue light, and blue also has a tranquillizing effect on emotionally disturbed patients. And according to the Lüscher color test, people who favor yellow are exhilarated, red excitable, and blue tranquil. Gazing at colors like pink, blue, and green can bring a wonderful state of calm to a troubled mind. It even works when you only do it in your imagination.

color your

mood

All too often we allow our choice of clothes to be dictated by fashion. But since color has such a powerful effect on our well-being it makes sense to be more selective and to listen to our feelings, likes, and dislikes. As a rule of thumb, don't buy anything that you don't feel totally comfortable in. It may be the latest fashion hit, but if the color or style does nothing for your well-being you will find yourself adding additional stress to your everyday life as well as your pocket.

I f you feel really stressed out and your nerves are getting the better of you, try the following visualization. See yourself walking down a path toward a gate. Open the gate and enter into the most beautiful garden you have ever seen. There are lovely flowers growing all around you. Inhale the wonderful scent and let your eyes rest on the magnificent display of color and shape. After a few moments open your eyes and return to your work more relaxed and refreshed. It's called day dreaming!

sunset soothers

" yesterday is but a memory and tomorrow is but a dream. "

Khalil Gibran

How often do you find ourselves reliving the past or anticipating the future? How many people spend sleepless nights worrying about things that might—or might not—happen tomorrow? The fact is you cannot change past experiences, nor can you plan exactly what the future will hold. The only time you have control over is the present moment. So let go of the past and take the future in your stride as it comes. That way you can live joyfully in the present moment, trusting you will have the strength and the ability to handle your challenges as and when they come.

After a long and stressful day it is vital for your well-being that you don't carry the troubles of that day into your night's sleep.

Allow your body to totally relax by first tensing all the muscles in your body and then consciously letting go. Breathe in through your nose, visualizing a white, shimmering light filling your body. Hold your breath for a few moments and allow that light to spread throughout your body. Then slowly breathe out, imagining that all your worries, upsets, and problems leave your body in a cloud of black smoke, coming out of your nose. Repeat this process three times, seeing the cloud of black smoke growing bigger in front of you on every out breath. Finally, visualize a beam of white light bursting forth from your forehead, and watch it dissolve the black cloud.

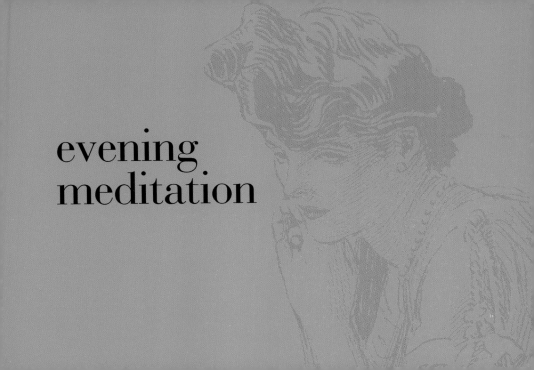

evening
meditation

drink your bedtime

A milky drink at bedtime is an effective inducer of sleep, thanks to an amino-acid present in milk called tryptophan. This stimulates the production of another chemical in the brain called serotonin, which calms the mind. According to the ancient Indian system of Ayurvedic medicine, adding spices to milk helps with digestion.

Try this simple recipe for hot nutmeg and ginger milk for a delicious end to your day: For each person put 1 cup lowfat or 2% milk in a small pan and bring to a boil. Reduce the heat and stir in $\frac{1}{2}$ teaspoon freshly grated nutmeg and $\frac{1}{2}$ teaspoon grated fresh gingerroot. Simmer for 5 minutes, then strain into a mug. Add honey to taste if desired.

Pleasant idleness

or sweet inactivity

wrapp'd

in guileless sleep

calm

and still.

Rev. Godfrey Thring

poem

for a good night's sleep, ritualize your day

If you're having trouble sleeping, it's important to re-establish normal sleep patterns as soon as possible. Creating a bedtime ritual will help you sleep sweetly. Go to bed at the same time every night and get up at the same time each day, including weekends. If you can't sleep after twenty minutes, get up and do something monotonous; the idea is to re-educate yourself that bed is for sleep and sex only!

If your evening peace is disturbed by thinking about the things you have not been able to complete during the day, don't wind yourself up by constantly thinking about them, make a list. As you write each item down, promise yourself you will do your best to deal with these issues first thing in the morning. Then let them go!

plant a scented
evening garden

The evening of the day is a time for rest and contemplation. What could be more pleasant than sitting on a patio on a summer evening enjoying the fragrance of a scented garden? Plant night-scented stock, vesper flower, phlox, and tobacco plants to create a scent-filled haven of peace away from the stresses and strains of everyday life.

Restoring more normal sleep patterns when we are stressed is vitally important, and a wide range of approaches can help to achieve this, ranging from the methods previously touched on—especially breathing retraining, relaxation, meditation, and visualization. Herbal teas such as valerian, passiflora, and camomile can safely ease feelings of undue tension, and are available at health food stores. The nutrients calcium, magnesium, and the B-vitamin complex can also help promote sleep.

restorative

measures

Orange blossom and lime flowers (linden blossoms) are well-known remedies for calming the mind and inducing sleep. Put one tablespoon dried lime flowers and one tablespoon dried orange blossom in a two-cup teapot. Pour over boiling water and cover. Leave to infuse for five minutes, then strain into a cup. Camomile, valerian, and passiflora are also wonderful herbs to gently aid sleep. Simply make an infusion and sip before going to bed.

forget the nightcap, sip herbal tea for a restful night's sleep

the**perfect**
bedroom

Any Feng-Shui advisor worth their money will tell you your bedroom should be as uncluttered as possible. Gentle, peaceful colors like blues and lilacs help to create an atmosphere conducive to good sleep. We should never carry anything that we wear during the day into our bedroom. The reason for this is that all these items carry the vibrations of hectic activity into a place where they don't belong. So it makes sense to take shoes, clothes, and jewelry off outside our bedroom and leave them there. Our ancestors must have known about this—that's why in olden days people had dressing rooms!

Make a strong infusion of fresh herbs by steeping them in a quart of boiling water until the water cools. Include as many of the following as possible: walnut leaves, bay, rosemary, lavender, sage, and lemon balm. Add a few drops of rosemary and bay essential oils and soak your feet for at least ten minutes.

a soothing
foot bath

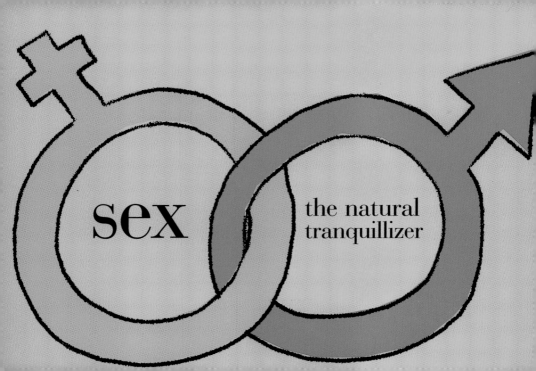

ex is not only fun but also extremely relaxing—it must be one of the most natural ways human beings are able to release tension and then find the comfort and closeness all relationships need. For sex to be relaxing and fulfilling there must not be any sense of hurry or interruptions, so make sure that children are tucked up in bed and the phone is off the hook. Then just allow yourself to relax as you go with gentle music, candlelight, and maybe some lovely scented massage oil to ease away the tensions of the day.

If you're having trouble dropping off to sleep, try adding a few drops of lavender essential oil to a warm bath before bed. Or put a few drops on a tissue and place near your pillow. Lavender is well known for its ability to aid sleep and alleviate stress.

sleep soundly with
lavender
a natural sedative

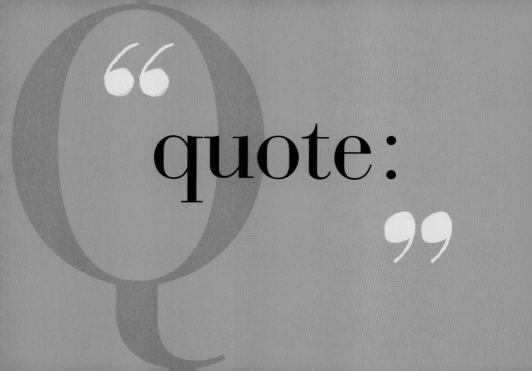

quote:

*a man can only do what he can do; but
if he does that each day he can sleep at
night and do it again the next day.*

Albert Schweitzer

take a walk

Everyone seems to know that walking in the woods or a beautiful park is one of the most stress-reducing activities we can enjoy. So why don't we do it more often? Sometimes it's hard to believe such simple actions can be so effective. But if you try it out for yourself you will soon be convinced of the benefits. Walking in the fresh air, surrounded by trees which provide the oxygen you need to breathe, and taking in the beauty and perfection of nature, will melt away anxiety and worries. Many people find it fills them with a sense of calm and peace, and reconnects them to the true rhythm of life.

in the woods